BASS GUITAR

BASS GUITAR

By Jim Gregory and Harvey Vinson.

Amsco Publications
London/New York/Sydney

International Standard Book Number: 0-8256-4061-X
Library of Congress Catalog Card Number: 73-75062

Distributed throughout the world by Music Sales Corporation:

24 East 22nd Street, New York, N.Y. 10010
8/9 Frith Street, London W1V 5TZ, England
27 Clarendon Street, Artarmon, Sydney NSW 2064

Photograph credits: L.F.I.

CONTENTS

INTRODUCTION

Of all the instruments used in pop and rock music, the electric bass has one of the shortest histories. The electric bass, as we now know it, has been in existence for only two decades. The aggression, sexuality, and sheer noise of the early rockers like Chuck Berry and Little Richard necessitated using an electric bass in "live" performances. When they recorded, however, these same bands frequently used the old stand-up, acoustic bass. This gives you an idea of how recently the electric bass has been accepted as a "legitimate" instrument by professional musicians.

Today, however, the electric bass player does more to control the tension and drive of the beat than any other musician. Giant banks of amplifiers with as many as 60 speakers are frequently used by the *bass player alone!** This, in contrast to the small, single-speaker bass amps used by early rock bands, demonstrates the elevation of the bass player in rock music.

The basic styles of rock, improvisation, rhythm theory, and more are discussed in this book.

---

* As Geezer Butler, the bass player for Black Sabbath (a particularly loud rock band), once said: "We're only in it for the volume."

FROM THE HEAD

The most important thing to remember about rock 'n' roll is that it's dance music. When you play rock, people dance; and dancing requires a strong, steady rhythm section. That's where you come in.

As the bass player in a rock band, it is your responsibility to keep the beat solid and moving. The bass player does more to control the tension and drive of the beat than any other member.

We'll get to playing as soon as you pick up on a few fundamentals of technique.

Electric bass guitar is part of the rhythm section usually consisting of drums and rhythm guitar (or keyboard). The enclosed 33⅓ rpm record provides such a rhythm section. Play the first side (band two) on your record player. This is the blues—or, more properly, rhythm and blues—and is what you'll be playing bass lines to for the first portion of this book. Listen to this selection a few times and then read on.

Although performing is done in a standing position, most bass guitarists practice sitting down.

Cross your legs and rest the rounded indentation of the bass on your right thigh. We'll worry about the left hand in a minute. With your right arm over the wide part of the bass, poise your right hand above the strings at the waist of the instrument.

Before playing, tune your bass guitar* to the record (side one, band one). This recording gives you the correct pitches for all four strings starting with the highest sounding string (1st string) and continuing to the lowest sounding string (4th string).**

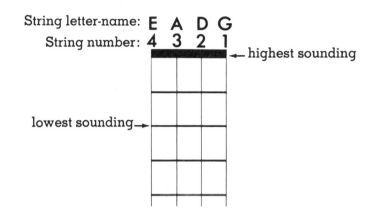

After your tuning reasonably matches the record's, play each of the strings a few times to get an idea of the pitch and location of each string. Say the letter-name of each string as you are playing it. For example, when you're playing***the 4th string, say out-loud, "E . . .E . . .E . . .etc." Continue this process with each string until you've played all four strings, making sure you only pluck one string at a time. You should be able to name the strings without hesitation.

Now start playing the A string (3rd string) in a slow but steady rhythm. As you're playing the A string, think about the location of the D string (2nd string) and try switching strings without losing the rhythm . . . and back to the A string again. Work on this remembering to keep the rhythm steady and *slow.* Using the same slow rhythm, start counting from 1 to 4 over and over:

Count: 1   2   3   4   1   2   3   4   1   2   3   4   1   2   3   4   etc.

While continuing to count, play the string indicated above each number. When you come to the end of the progression, start counting and playing immediately from the beginning again.

If you're without an electric bass guitar or amp, see the Appendix for advice on equipment brand names, financial hints, etc. A guitar cable and an adjustable guitar strap are the other pieces of miscellaneous equipment you need.

**Since there will be times when you won't have your record player with you, detailed tuning instructions are presented later in the book.*

***For the time being, use either the index or middle finger of the right hand to pluck the strings.*

Blues Progression in A

Play:	A	A	A	A	A	A	A	A	A	A	A	A	A	A	A	A
Count:	1	2	3	4	1	2	3	4	1	2	3	4	1	2	3	4

	D	D	D	D	D	D	D	D	A	A	A	A	A	A	A	A
	1	2	3	4	1	2	3	4	1	2	3	4	1	2	3	4

	E	E	E	E	D	D	D	D	A	A	A	A	E	E	E	E
	1	2	3	4	1	2	3	4	1	2	3	4	1	2	3	4

*Repeat from
the beginning.*

After playing this progression a few times on the slow side, speed it up and practice it at a quick tempo. It is an important progression to spend time with.

The progression you've been playing is known as the *blues progression* or simply *blues* (also known as the *standard progression*). Originally a chordal vehicle for early Negro sorrow-songs, the blues progression and style attained international recognition in the mid-1910's by such composers as W.C. Handy *(St. Louis Blues)*. Not only is this progression the foundation of jazz but, more important, it is the foundation of rock. Every list of top rock tunes always includes songs based on this progression. Rhythm and blues bands (Fats Domino, Chuck Berry) and straight blues bands (Butterfield Blues Band, B.B. King, Albert King) rely mostly on this progression. The technique and style of today's rock scene and the technique and style of rock bass guitar is derived from this progression.

Let's go back to the record. The cut that you've been listening to (side one, band two) is entitled *Blues Progression in A*. This is the same progression you've been working on. Try playing along with the record following the preceding outline of the blues progression. First start counting with the record. The second time you count the number "1" begin playing.*

Play:					A	A	A	A	A	A	A	A	etc.
Count:	1	2	3	4	1	2	3	4	1	2	3	4	etc.

\begin playing here

Notice that each string change is preceded by a short drum roll.

If your playing doesn't sound right to you, practice the progression from the outline without the record. Make sure you are:

1) playing the right strings,
2) playing with your bass in tune
3) not speeding up (don't play faster than the record).

If it sounds all right, go on to the next chapter.

---

* *Counting before you start playing cues the band to the tempo of the song.*

BASICS

Now that you know how the blues progression sounds, let's learn how it is notated. The electric bass has four strings, and the tablature system used in this book (based on a combination of the Spanish and French tablature systems) uses four lines:*

Vertical lines (called bar lines) divide the staff into measures:

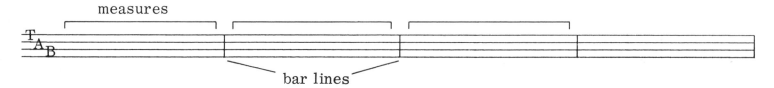

A measure is a unit of time usually consisting of four beats (or counts).

Each of the four lines of the tablature staff represents a bass string: the top line stands for the highest sounding string (G string), the next line stands for the next string down (D string), the next-to-bottom line stands for the A string, and the bottom line stands for the lowest sounding string (E string).

Playing from tablature is an old and honorable tradition. Even as far back as the 15th century, organ music was commonly notated in tablature. In the 16th century, almost all lute music was scored in tablature. The immense popularity of tablature in the past can be accorded to one primary reason: that reading music from tablature is easy.

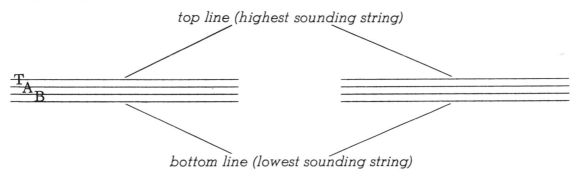

top line (highest sounding string)

bottom line (lowest sounding string)

An "o" on the tablature staff indicates that you play a specific string *open* or unfingered. For example, an "o" on the top line means that you play the highest sounding string open.

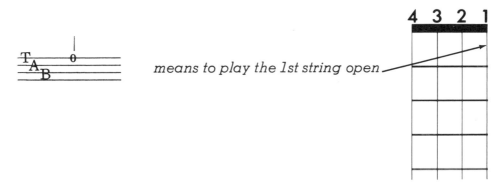

means to play the 1st string open

An "o" on the 2nd line indicates that you play the 2nd string open.

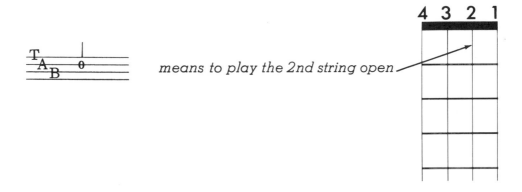

means to play the 2nd string open

Using this system, here is the entire *Blues Progression in A* from the first chapter. Notice how much easier it is to read.

Blues Progression in A #2

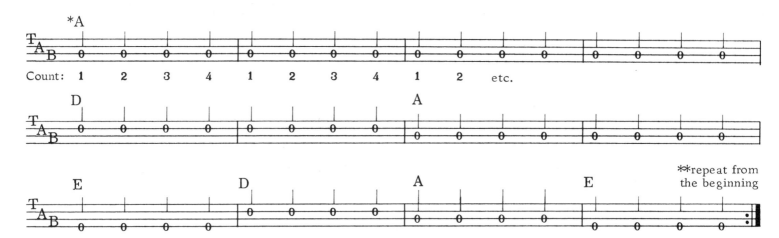

Count: 1   2   3   4   1   2   3   4   1   2   etc.

Play the progression through a few times using this outline (with or without the record). Keep your eyes on the page, not on your right hand. Compare it to the previous blues outline.

Count the number of measures in *Blues Progression in A;* you'll find it to be 12 measures (or bars) long. If you repeat the progression, the length is 12 times two. Although the length of the blues progression varied originally from 8 to 16 bars, it has become fixed by today's rock players at 12 bars. It is referred to as "12 bar blues" no matter how many repeats you take.

---

* *The letters above the tablature staff indicate the chord choices for the rhythm instruments. Once a chord is indicated, that chord is used until a new one is called for. In this case, the A chord is played for the first four measures.*

** *Go back to the first measure and play the 3rd string open on the next "1" count.*

14

RIFFS-I

Let's learn a moving bass line. First, reexamine the tablature staff. Arabic numbers on the tablature staff indicate the specific string and fret positions to play. A "5" on the bottom line indicates that you play the lowest sounding string fretted at the 5th fret. Left hand fingering appears immediately below the tab notes:

means to play the 4th string, 5th fret with the index finger:

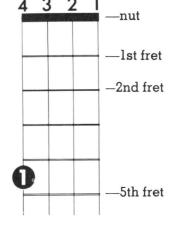

While fingering the above note, the left hand looks like this:

Note that the string is depressed immediately behind the 5th fret by the tip of the 1st finger.* Also, that the thumb points towards the tuning pegs.

---

* Both left and right hand nails must be clipped short.

A "7" on the next line up indicates that you play the 3rd string fretted at the 7th fret.

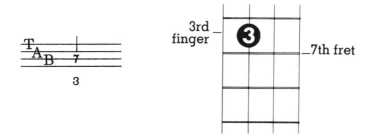

A "5" on the 2nd line from the top has you playing the 2nd string fretted at the 5th fret.

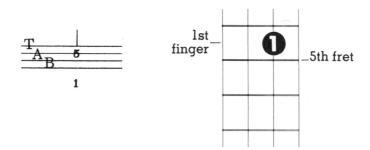

A "7" on the 2nd line employs the 2nd string fretted at the 7th fret.

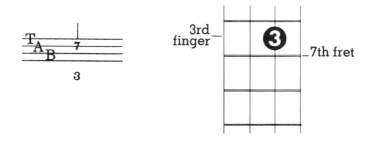

These four notes can be combined to play a bass guitar riff.* Count from 1 to 4 playing one note on each beat.

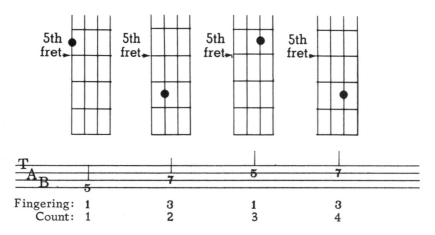

———————————

* A riff is a short, melodic phrase which is usually repeated.

Play it through a few times until you can play it with ease:

| Fingering: | 1 | 3 | 1 | 3 | 1 | 3 | 1 | 3 | 1 | 3 | 1 | 3 |
| Count: | 1 | 2 | 3 | 4 | 1 | 2 | 3 | 4 | 1 | etc. | | |

In preparation for the moving bass line, move the entire riff over one string, and play it a few times (the first note of the riff is now on the 3rd string). Keep the same left hand fingering.

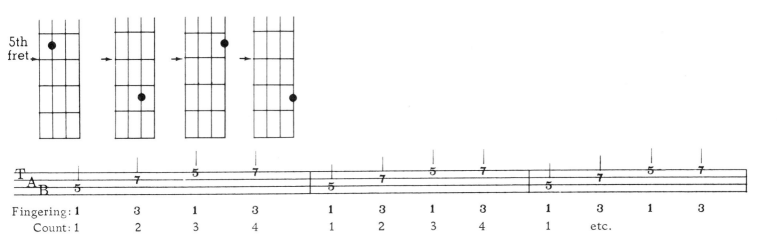

| Fingering: | 1 | 3 | 1 | 3 | 1 | 3 | 1 | 3 | 1 | 3 | 1 | 3 |
| Count: | 1 | 2 | 3 | 4 | 1 | 2 | 3 | 4 | 1 | etc. | | |

Keeping the first note of the riff on the 3rd string, move the riff up two frets (towards you) and play it a few times. After learning the riff in this position, you'll be able to play the first moving bass line.

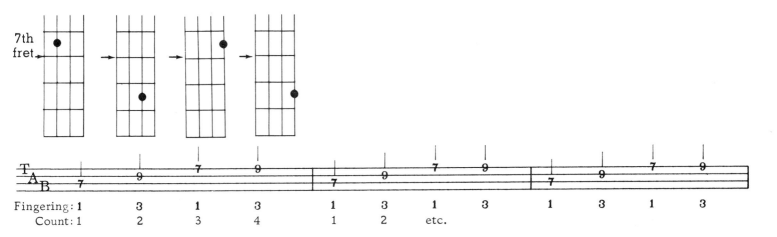

| Fingering: | 1 | 3 | 1 | 3 | 1 | 3 | 1 | 3 | 1 | 3 | 1 | 3 |
| Count: | 1 | 2 | 3 | 4 | 1 | 2 | etc. | | | | | |

Now for the bass line. Look it over before you start playing. Notice that the riff changes position at each chord change. Practice the bass line a few times and then try it with the rhythm background of the *Blues Progression in A* (side one). The chord symbols above the tab staff tell you where you are in relation to the blues progression.

Blues Progression in A #3

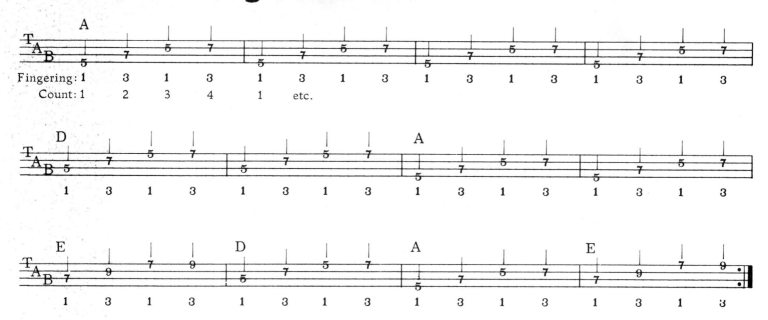

The repetition of a melodic riff in the blues progression runs throughout the history of rock. Even in the 1920's, a full 30 years before rock, barrelhouse pianists were pounding out 12 bar boogie-woogie with its repetitive left hand (bass note) patterns. The chordal structure of the blues lends itself to this concept. Used from the early days of rock (Bill Doggett's *Honky Tonk*) to the late 60's (the Cream's *Sunshine Of Your Love*), the riff repetition in the blues progression has become a standard rock idiom.

RIFFS-II

Once you start playing bass riffs, dozens of riff ideas will start popping into your head. Riff bass playing follows an easily understandable formula which partially accounts for the popularity of this style of playing. It only takes one four note riff to get you through the entire blues progression! First, take a one measure riff* that can be played against an A chord:

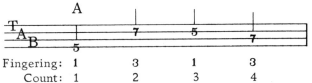

Play this one measure riff whenever an A chord appears in the blues progression.

Blues Progression in A #4

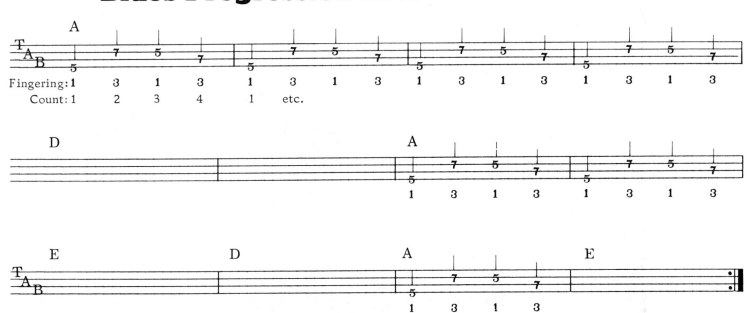

This riff is a slight variation of the first one you learned.

Play the same riff with the same fingering starting on the 3rd string everytime a D chord appears.

Blues Progression in A #4

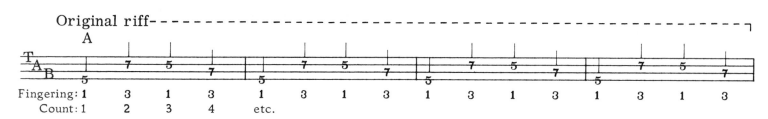

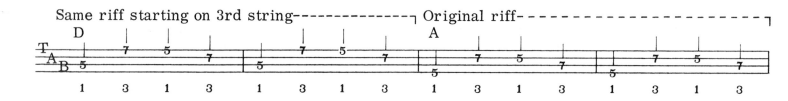

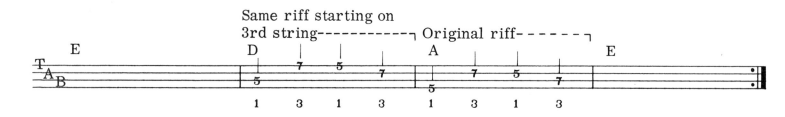

With the riff starting on the 3rd string, raise it two frets. Play the riff in this position everytime an E chord appears in the blues progression. Make sure you understand this formula before going on.

Blues Progression in A #4

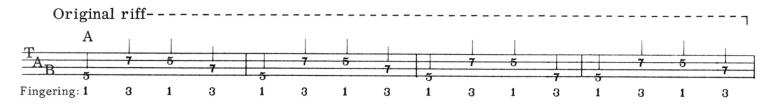

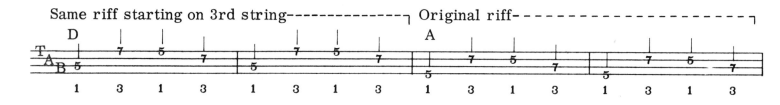

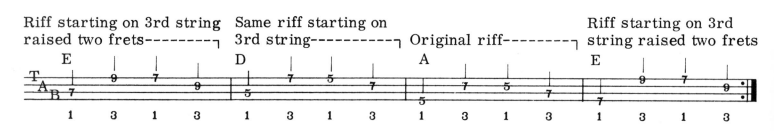

So now you have another bass line to play with the record. Compare this one to the bass line in the previous chapter.

To create a new bass line, all you need is a different one measure riff. Once you have a new riff, use the formula presented in this chapter to construct the bass line. Play this next riff a few times. The first note is repeated so take care.

Fingering: 1   1   3   1
Count: 1   2   3   4

Play a solo using this riff. For variety, play the bass line from the previous chapter for the first chorus (first time through the blues progression), the second bass line for the second chorus, and the last bass line for the third chorus.

For a new bass line learn this riff. The left hand fingering is a little different than in the others.

Fingering: 2   1   4   1
Count: 1   2   3   4

There are many different riffs you could memorize but a much better idea is to make up some of your own. For now, the only requirement is that the first riff should sound good played against an A chord. Play the A string of the bass a few times to get the sound of A in your ears and then compose your own riff. You'll have an easier time of it if you'll make this the first note:

first note

After you've created a good riff, the rest is easy.

RHYTHM AND STUFF

Up to now, you've been playing one note on each beat. Because of its time value this note is a quarter note and is identified by a single stem.

Quarter notes—one on each beat

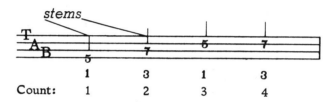

Another important time value is the eighth note. Eighth notes are played two on each beat and are connected by a beam. Count "&" between each beat when playing this new rhythm.

Eighth notes—two on each beat

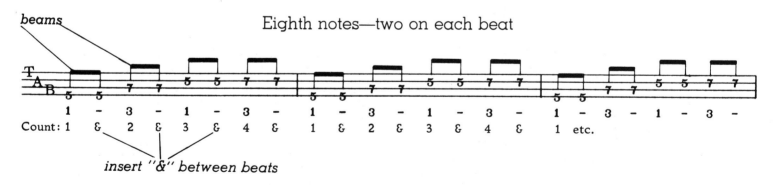

insert "&" between beats

Right hand technique is important when you play eighth notes. The strings of the bass are plucked by the index and middle fingers of the right hand.* With the thumb resting on the 4th string, play the 2nd string with the index finger. As the index finger clears the 2nd string, allow it to rest on the 3rd string.

After playing the 2nd string, the index finger rests on the 3rd string. After playing the 2nd string, the middle finger rests on the 3rd string.

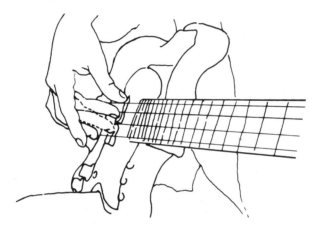

Follow the same technique when playing the 1st, 2nd, and 3rd strings. When playing the 4th string, hold the thumb clear.**

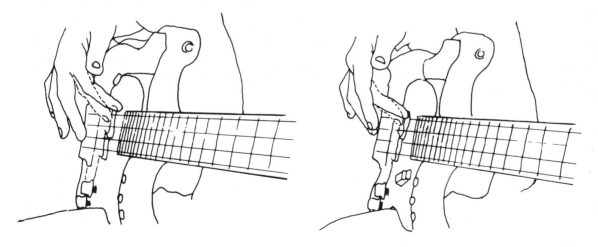

Many studio bass players favor using the pick because of the crispness of the attack. In rock, however, the use of the pick causes the bass to lose some of its punch.

* * Both left and right hand nails must be clipped short.

When playing this eighth note riff, use the middle finger (m) on the beat. On the "&" between the beats use the index finger (i). Here's the riff with the right hand fingering:

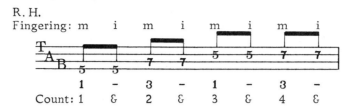

And, of course, a one measure eighth note riff functions in the bass line formula the same way as a one measure quarter note riff. Play the next bass line to better understand this. It uses a slight (but improved) variation of the last eighth note riff. Pay particular attention to the right hand fingerings.

Blues Progression in A #5

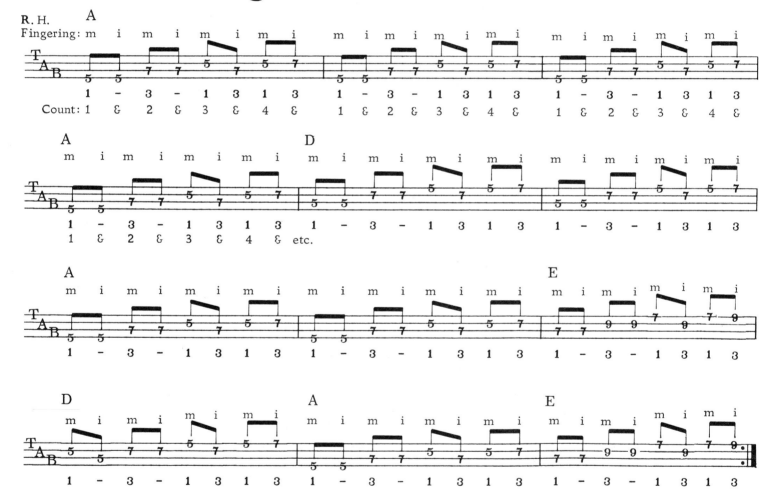

Learn this next eighth note riff for a new bass line. Watch the left and right hand fingerings carefully.

After you have it in your fingers, use it with the formula for a new bass line.

Quarter notes and eighth notes are often used together in the same one measure riff. In this next riff, play eighth notes on the 2nd and 4th beats and quarter notes on the 1st and 3rd beats.

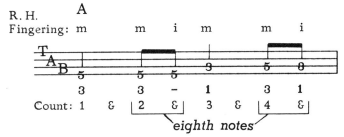

Using the last riff you can play still another bass line with the record.

An important device that improves the rhythm of a riff is the tie: ⌣ . When two notes of the same pitch are tied together, *sustain the sound of the first note through the time value of the second note.* Suppose you had this to play:

Here's the same riff with the first and second notes tied together. Sustain the sound of the first note, do not play the second note. The next note you would play is on the "&" after the "2." Try it.

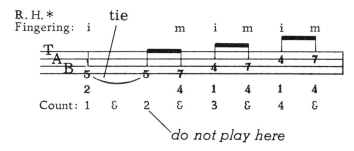

Play the last riff with the record.

This next riff makes use of two ties. The notes on both the "2" and the "4" beats are tied to the previous notes. Practice quite slowly making sure you're playing the right time values.

Using the last riff, play a bass line with the record. Follow all fingerings with care.

This riff begins with the index finger (i) so take care.

Blues Progression in A #6

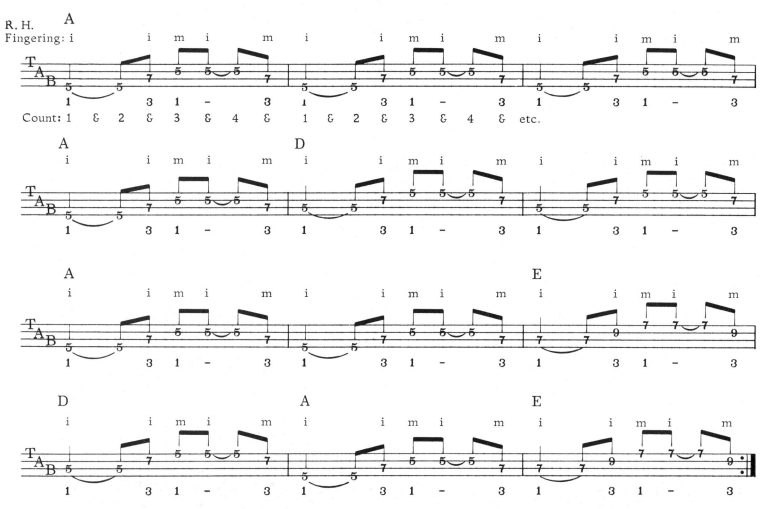

MORE STUFF

One of the important techniques used in building a rock bass line is the concept of question and answer. This can be done by extending the length of the riff from one measure to two measures. Play this two measure riff:

1st measure (question) .... 2nd measure (answer) ...

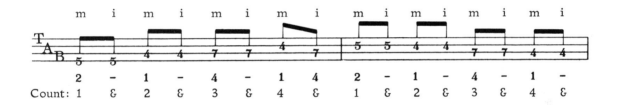

The first measure is answered by the second measure. Clearly, these two measures compliment each other and make a unified musical statement.

A two measure riff works similarly to the one measure riff in the blues progression. Play the two measure riff whenever an A chord appears in the blues progression. When the progression calls for only one measure of A (measure 11), play only the first measure of the riff.

Blues Progression in A #7

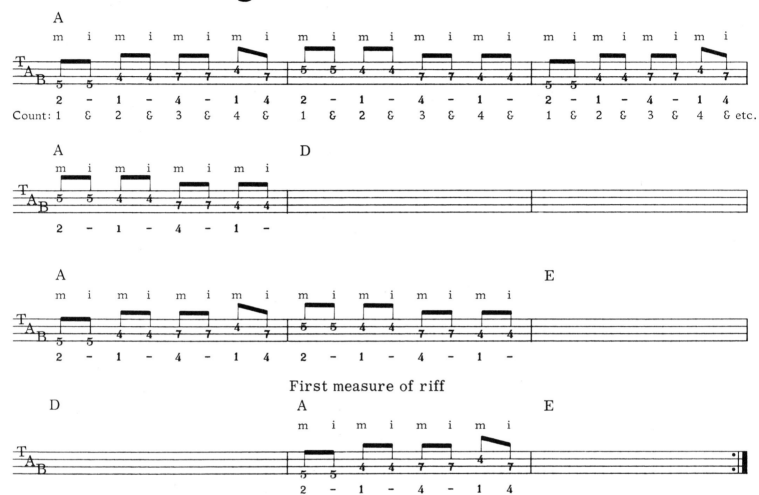

First measure of riff

Whenever a D chord appears, play the same two measure riff starting on the 3rd string. When the blues progression calls for only one measure of D, as in measure 10, play the first measure of the riff. For the E chord use only the first measure of the riff (raised two frets, starting on the 3rd string). After you're familiar with the construction of the bass line, play it with the record.

Blues Progression in A #7

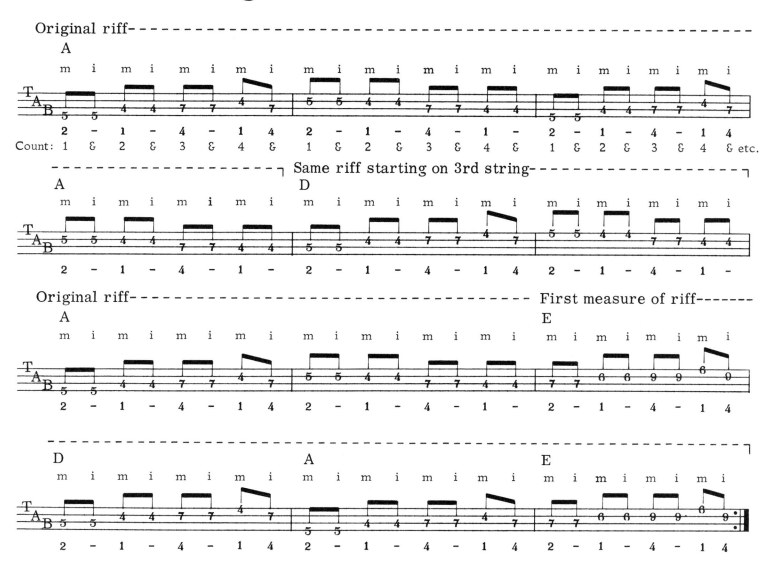

Here's another two measure riff. This one makes use of the tie. Practice it quite slowly at first making sure not to play on the "2" of the second measure.

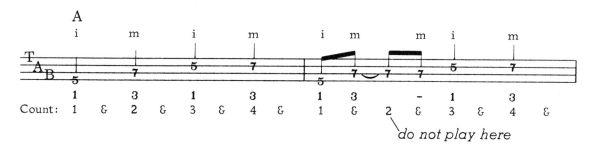

After you've learned the last riff, play another solo using the two measure riff technique. Be sure to play only the first measure of the riff in the last four measures of the progression.

Try this more sophisticated two measure riff for a new bass line.

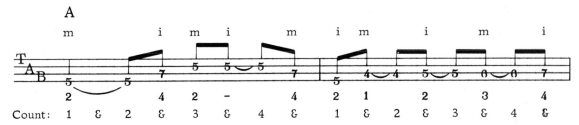

Here's the last riff using the new formula. If your left hand starts to ache, relax for a few minutes and try the bass line again. One other thing— the last measure of the blues progression (12th measure) frequently breaks the usual sequence to add interest as the progression returns to the first measure. The following bass line illustrates this technique.

Blues Progression in A #8

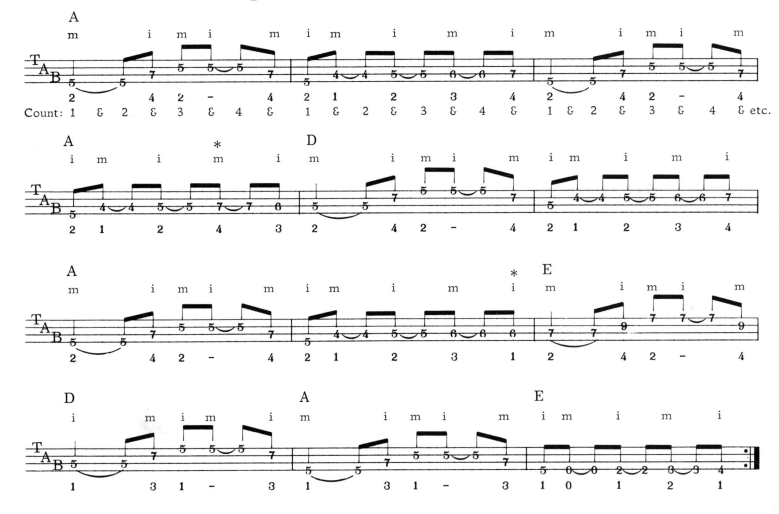

A slight alteration in the second measure of the riff makes the transition to the chord changes musically more convincing. Feel free to make any such alterations that occur to you.

For a new bass line to play with the record, learn the next eighth note riff. This riff has an American Indian flavor and can be quite driving.

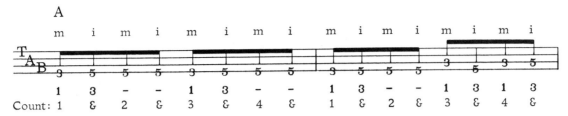

Quarter notes can also be tied together effectively. In the following riff, do not play on the "2" or the "4" of the first measure. The effect is a relaxed first measure followed by a tense, syncopated* second measure. This type of contrast can be quite exciting.

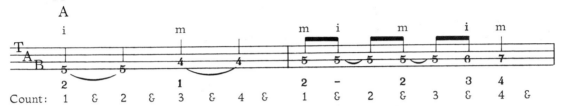

Here's a complete blues using the last two bar riff. The last four bars are altered slightly in order to maintain tension.

Blues Progression in A #9

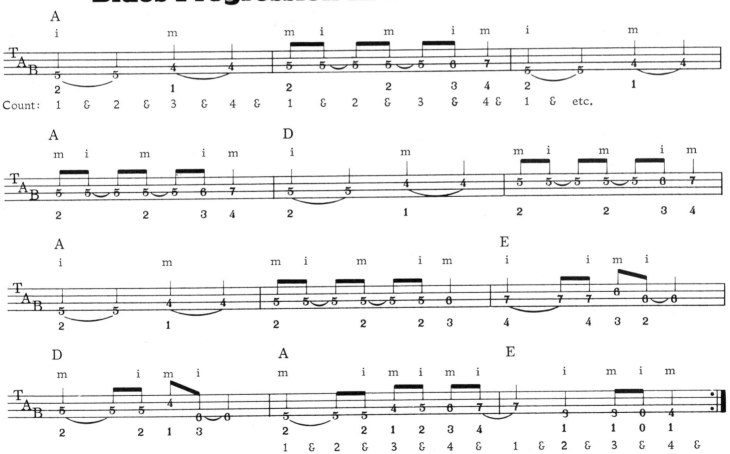

Syncopation is any deliberate upsetting or displacing of the regular pulse or rhythm. In the second measure of the example, you play only on the 1st and 4th downbeats with the 2nd and 3rd beats syncopated or displaced.

31

The next two bar riff was originated by Jack Bruce of Cream and later used by many other bands including Jim Fiedler of Blood Sweat & Tears.

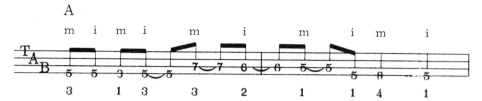

The number of people that have danced and snapped their fingers to the following bass line is astronomical. Learn this line well and you can apply for your union card next week.

Blues Progression in A #10

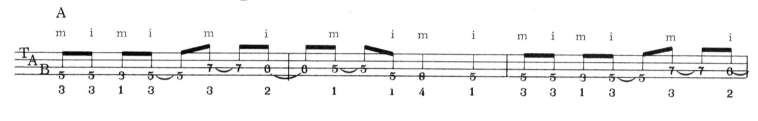

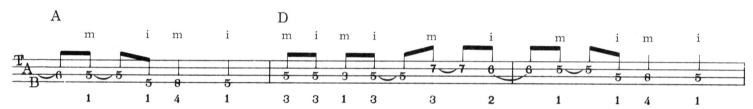

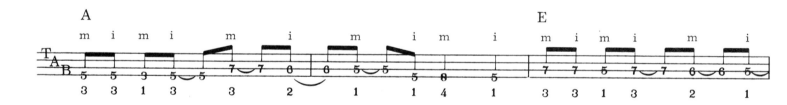

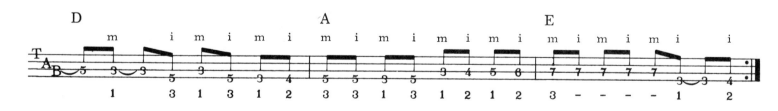

Try making up 2nd measures of your own and tagging them on to some of your favorite one measure riffs presented earlier. Keep in mind that the 2nd measure of the riff should "answer" and compliment the 1st measure.

GETTING DOWN TO TUNING UP

Since there will be times when you won't have your tuning record (or record player), you must learn other ways to tune your bass. When you're playing along and something just doesn't sound right, you can almost bet that your bass is out of tune. The more you play with a tuned bass, the easier you can tell when it is out of tune. The person who suffers the most from an out-of-tune instrument is you and your ears. So keep your instrument in tune!

When you're playing in a group, tune your bass to the other instruments in the band. If there is an organ or piano in the band, tune to that since its pitch is fixed. Otherwise, choose the instrument that is closest to being perfectly in tune and use that as your standard.

When tuning to an organ (or a piano), the 1st string on the bass (G) corresponds to the G an eleventh below middle C (the 10th white to the left of middle C). Here is a diagram which shows you how to find the notes you'll need:

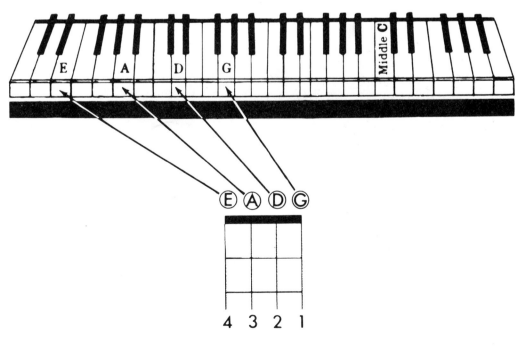

By pushing the far right foot-pedal of the piano down with your foot and striking a note, the sound of that note will be sustained. Strike the key corresponding to the 1st string (G). While the tone is still ringing, play the 1st string and compare the sounds. Do they sound similar? If the 1st string is sharper (higher in pitch) or flatter (lower) than the sound of the piano, adjust the pitch of the 1st string by turning the appropriate tuning peg.

The tuning peg will turn more easily going down in pitch than going up. As you turn the peg, keep plucking the string gently with your right hand thumb so you can hear the pitch of the string changing. If the sound from the piano dies out too soon, strike it again as you compare sounds while you tune the string. If the pitches don't seem to match as you continually turn and turn that peg—stop and be sure you are:

    1) playing the right piano key,
    2) playing the right string, and
    3) turning the peg in the right direction.

In similar fashion, tune the other three strings.

When tuning to a guitar,* the four lowest sounding strings of the guitar correspond to the four strings of the bass. The sound is an octave higher but it's easy for your ears to make the adjustment. The 3rd string of the guitar open corresponds to the 1st string of the bass open.

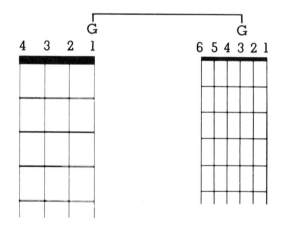

The 4th string of the guitar corresponds to the 2nd string of the bass.

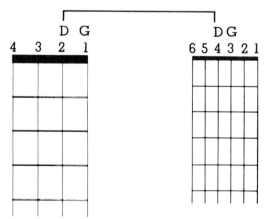

The two lowest sounding strings of the bass correspond similarly to the two lowest sounding strings of the guitar.

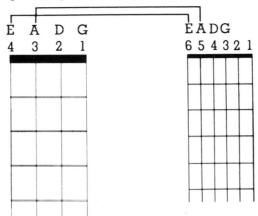

The most widely used method of tuning is unfortunately the most difficult. This method starts by assuming that the 1st string (G) is on pitch.* If it seems too high (tight), loosen the string a bit; if it seems too low loose and buzzing), turn the peg to tighten the string.

When the 1st string sounds all right to you, fret the 2nd string at the 5th fret. At the same time, pluck the 2nd string—the note you should get is G, the same note as the 1st string open. Tune the 2nd string.

same sound as

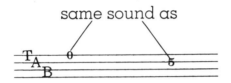

When the 2nd string is in tune, fret the 3rd string at the 5th fret. Pluck the 3rd string—the note you should get is D, the same note as the 2nd string open.

same sound as

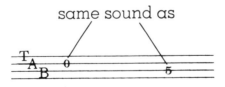

Tune the 4th string in a similar fashion.

same sound as

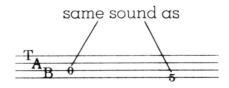

---

* Tune to the piano, the low G from the guitar, or a pitch pipe.

When you've done all that, play some of the riffs you know to check your tuning. You might have to go over your tuning a few times until you get the right sounds.

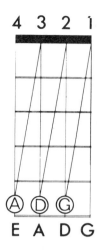

Most professional bass players use a system of tuning that employs harmonics. Place the 3rd finger of the left hand directly above the 7th fret of the 1st string. Lightly touch the string (without pressing down) with the finger and pluck the string at the same time.*

The sound produced has an almost flute like quality. Worn or "dead" strings may not produce a harmonic at all. The harmonic is notated:

The corresponding harmonic on the 2nd string is produced at the 5th fret. The idea is to get both harmonics sounding at the same time so you can compare the sounds and adjust the tuning.

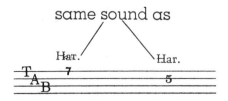

_____

* *Harmonics are easier to hear with a high treble setting on the bass (or amp).*

The harmonic at the 5th fret of the 3rd string corresponds to the harmonic at the 7th fret of the 2nd string.

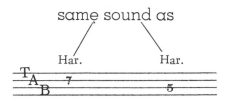

The 4th string relates to the 3rd string similarly.

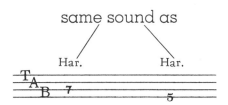

This is a difficult method of tuning so if you have problems with it, don't be upset. It would be worth the effort to get a bass playing friend to demonstrate it to you if you can't get it together.

THE TRIPLET TRIP

Listen to the 2nd cut on side two of the record to hear the blues played with a different rhythmic feel (the cut entitled *Triplet Blues in A*). In the counting preceding the actual playing notice that each beat is subdivided into three parts:

Count: *1* 2 3 *2* 2 3 *3* 2 3 *4* 2 3 *1*

playing begins here

Try counting this new rhythm accenting the first number in each beat.

Using this rhythm you can play three notes on each beat. This figure is called a *triplet* and is notated by three eighth notes with the number "3" written above the connecting beam.

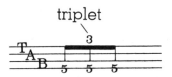

triplet

Count and play this example, lightly plucking the 4th string three times on each beat.

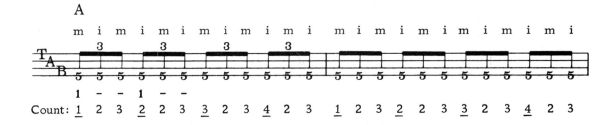

The *Triplet Blues in A* also illustrates a popular variation of the standard progression. Analyze the notated outline. Although the same chords are used (A, A , D , E), they change more frequently. This increased number of chord changes suggest more interesting bass lines. Play the progression through a few times using this simple bass line and then try it with the record.

Triplet Blues in A #1

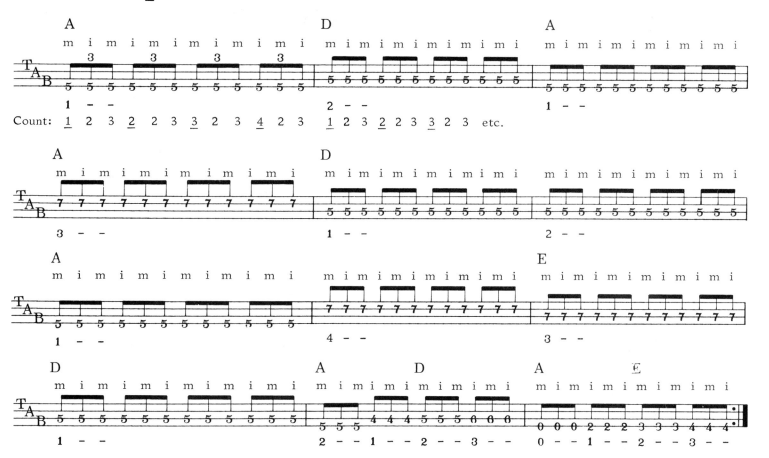

The treatment of the riff in this chordal version of the blues progression is quite similar to the formula you've been using. Since the D7 chord appears in the 2nd measure, switch the riff to the 3rd string for that measure. The rest of the progression is handled the same way except in the 11th and 12th measures.

Learn this one measure riff in preparation for a new bass line in triplets.

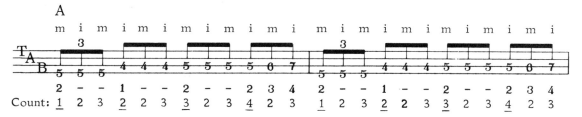

Now for the bass line. The last few notes of a riff are frequently altered to accommodate chord changes. Pay particular attention to the 4th and the 8th through the 12th measures. This is a nice bass line so spend some time with it.

Triplet Blues in A #2

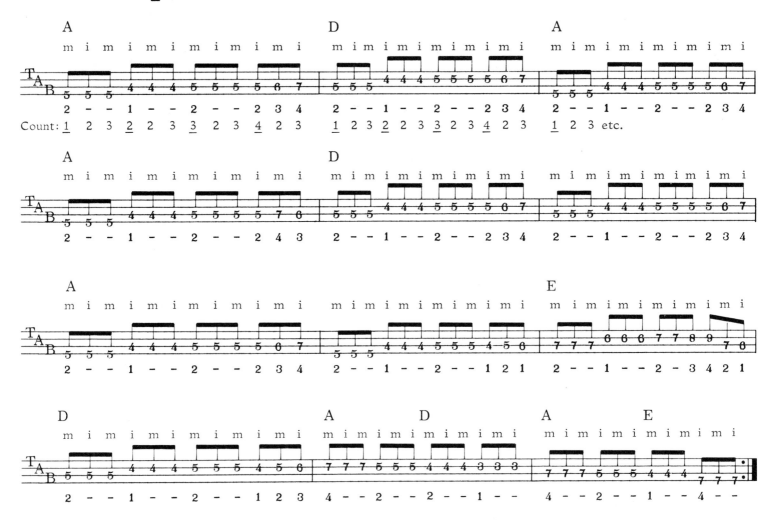

If you had trouble playing the last bass line fast enough to accompany the record, work on the next two scale exercises for awhile and then go back to the bass line. In any case, work on these exercises. They will increase the speed and agility of both your left and right hands. Practice them *very slowly* at first.

A Blues Scale
Exercise #1

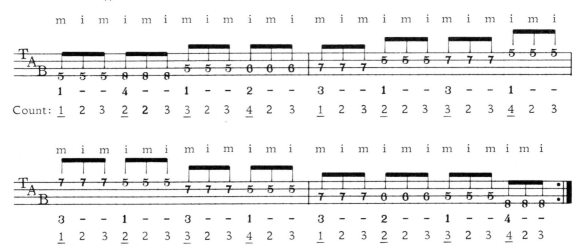

The last exercise is the A blues scale. A fingerboard diagram of the scale looks like this:

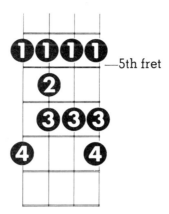

It is very important to have this scale "in your fingers" as many rock bass lines employ only notes derived from this scale. After you've mastered it, try this one.

A Blues Scale
Exercise #2

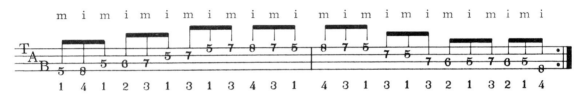

For variation, play the exercises starting with the index (i) finger.

Exercise #3

Exercise #4

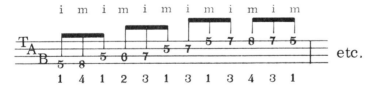

Try these scales starting at different frets (i.e. the 3rd and 8th frets). These exercises are excellent to play before you begin your daily practice. They warm-up your hands and get you in the mood to play.

A very popular rock rhythm based on the triplet is the shuffle rhythm. The shuffle rhythm is achieved by *not playing* on the "2" of the triplet figure. An eighth note rest ⅞ inserted here indicates this rhythm:

To better understand the shuffle rhythm, play the next example. You'll get the feel of this new rhythm quicker if you'll accent the first note of each beat.

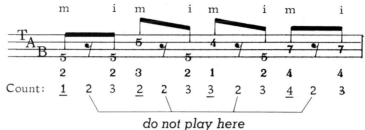

do not play here

After you master the last riff, play the next bass line with the record.

Triplet Blues in A #3

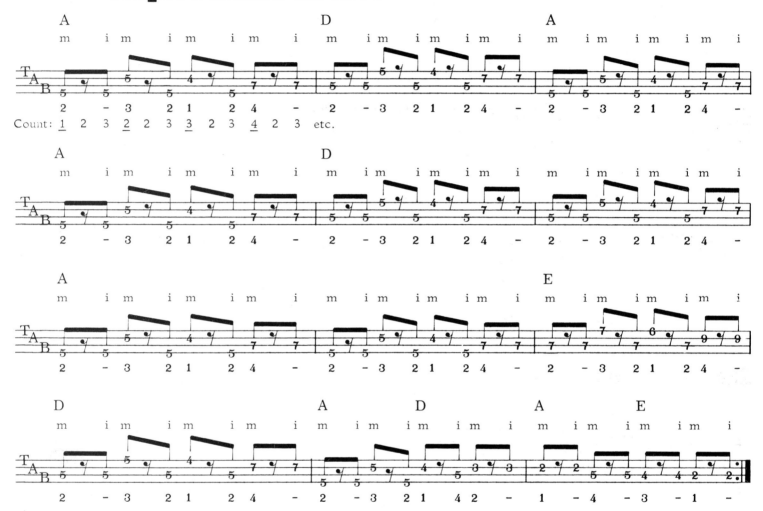

Occasionally the shuffle rhythm and the triplet rhythm are played together as in the next riff:

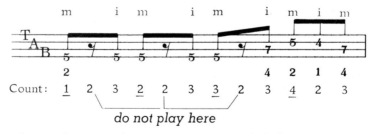

do not play here

Play the next bass line with care as many of the connecting runs are altered.

Triplet Blues in A #4

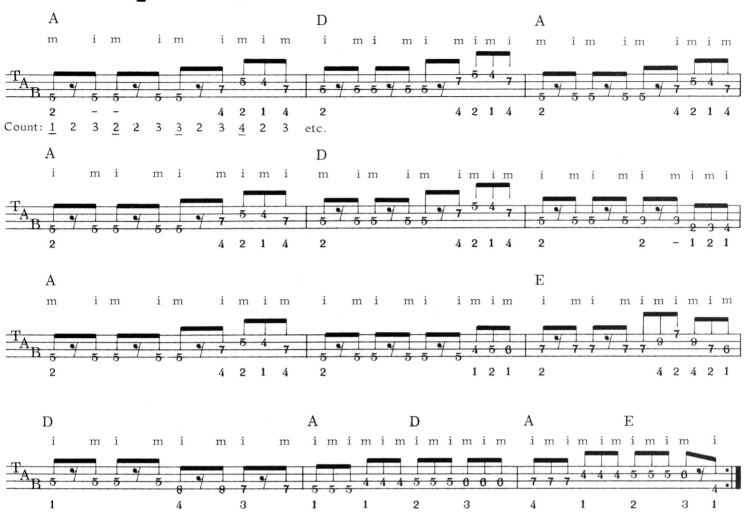

Many of the eighth notes riffs you've learned can be effectively played with the shuffle rhythm. For instance:

Eighth Note Rhythm

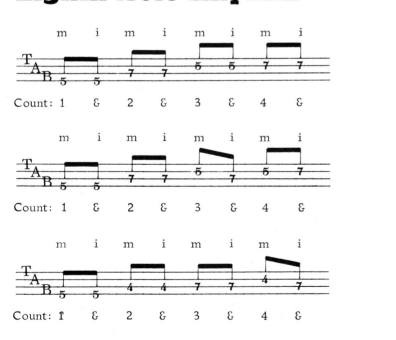

Shuffle Rhythm

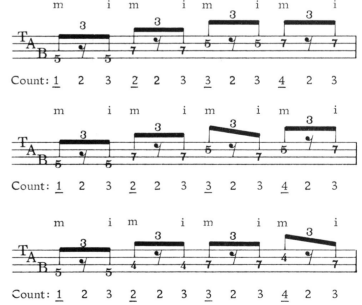

Try a couple of bass lines using some of these shuffle rhythm riffs.

RHYTHM RIFFS

New bass lines can be created by considering only the rhythm of a riff. First, examine this riff:

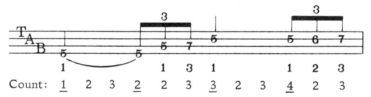

If we followed the riff formula, you would simply move the entire riff over to the 3rd string:

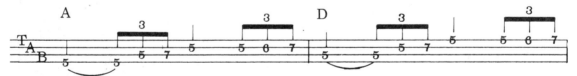

Try tapping out only the rhythm of the riff without actually playing it. The rhythm looks like this in notation:

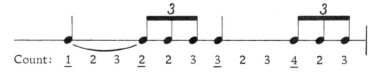

By using the riff's rhythm as a basis, the second measure could be stated like so:

Note that the rhythm in both measures is identical. However, the melodic texture of the bass line in the second measure is significantly different than in the first measure. The concept, then, is to duplicate the rhythm of the first measure in the succeeding measures.

This rhythm riff idea plugs easily into the one measure riff formula. Instead of following the exact melody and rhythm in each measure, use only the rhythm. We'll get into a complete bass line using this idea, but first some technique.

When two notes of the same pitch are tied together, sustain the sound of the first note through the time value of the second note. When two notes of *different pitches* are tied together, play only the first note. While the string is still ringing, hammer-down the indicated left hand finger to make the second note sound. Don't play the second note with the right hand—the left hand alone produces the sound.

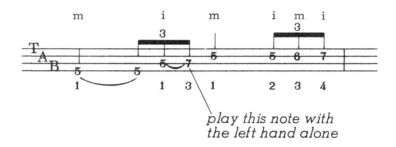

play this note with the left hand alone

This technique is called a *hammer-on* and is quite effective.

The next bass line is in the style of Jack Cassidy of Jefferson Airplane, Jefferson Starship, etc. Although the rhythm riff is not duplicated exactly throughout the blues, the rhythmic outline of the riff is consistently present. Emphasis on the first note in each measure gives the entire bass line logic and unity.

Triplet Blues in A #5

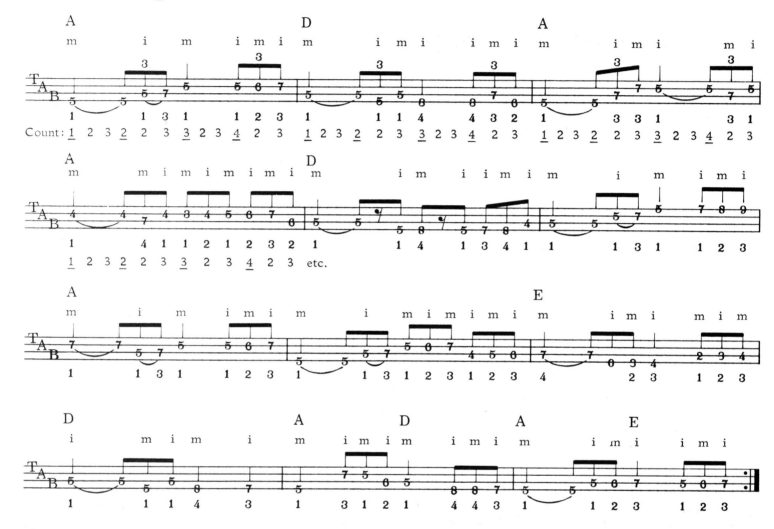

The two measure rhythm riff functions similarly to the two measure melodic riff. Examine and play this riff:

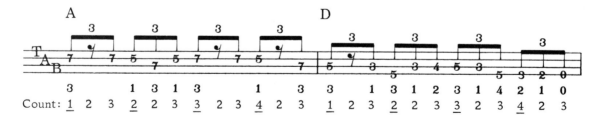

Here's the rhythmic outline of the riff:

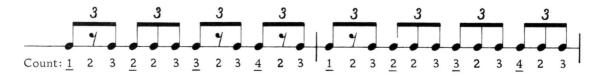

The next bass line illustrates this technique. It is again in the style of Jack Cassidy. Try playing the last bass line and immediately going into this one. Notice that the melodic figure stated in the last half of the third measure and the beginning of the fourth measure is restated in the seventh measure. This further solidifies the line. The starting note of the riff is on the 7th fret of the 2nd string which is a duplicate of the note produced by the 4th string at the 5th fret.

Triplet Blues in A #6

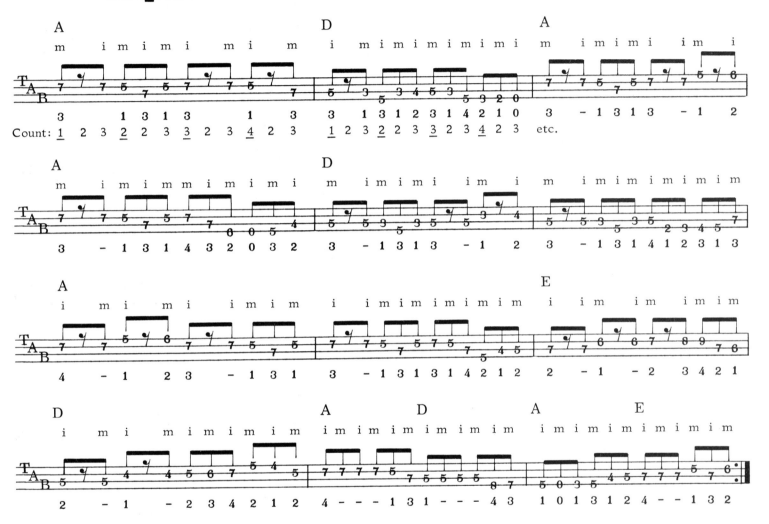

WALKING BASS

A style of bass playing derived from straight blues bands* is the walking bass. The walking bass avoids the repetition of the riff style by approaching the bass line as a horizontal concept. The bass line moves slowly (often in quarter notes) supporting the chord changes in a less direct way. This style of playing allows the bass player more melodic creativity in his approach to a song. Try this walking bass with the *Triplet Blues in A* cut on the record.

Walking Bass #1

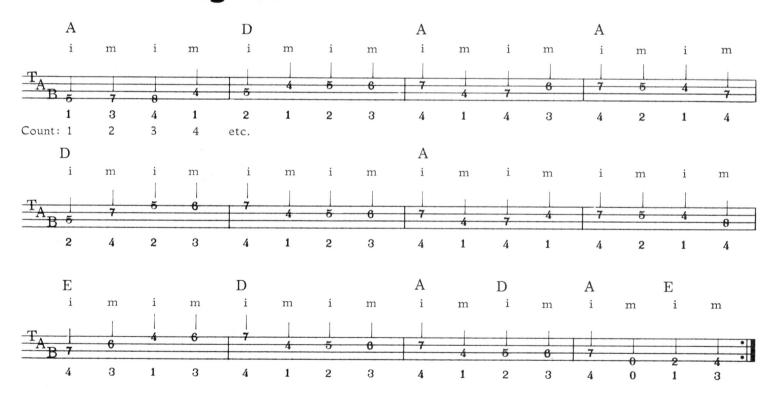

Bands that rely on the blues progression as the exclusive chordal vehicle for their material.

The triplet and shuffle rhythms are often used with the regular quarter note rhythm to increase the interest of the line. The next bass line, in the style of Leo Lauchie (the great B.B. King's main bass-man), illustrates this technique. Note that this increased activity also makes the chord changes more convincing.

Walking Bass #2

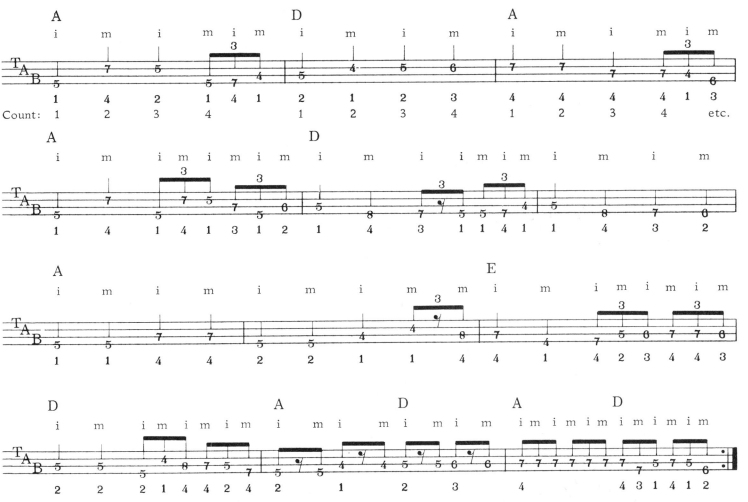

Since there is an absence of defined rhythmic patterns in the walking bass, the melodic texture of the line becomes more important. This partially explains the popularity of this style of playing with jazz bass players. The effect is a graceful feel with melodic statements created both by the lead instrument and the bass simultaneously.

Walking Bass #3

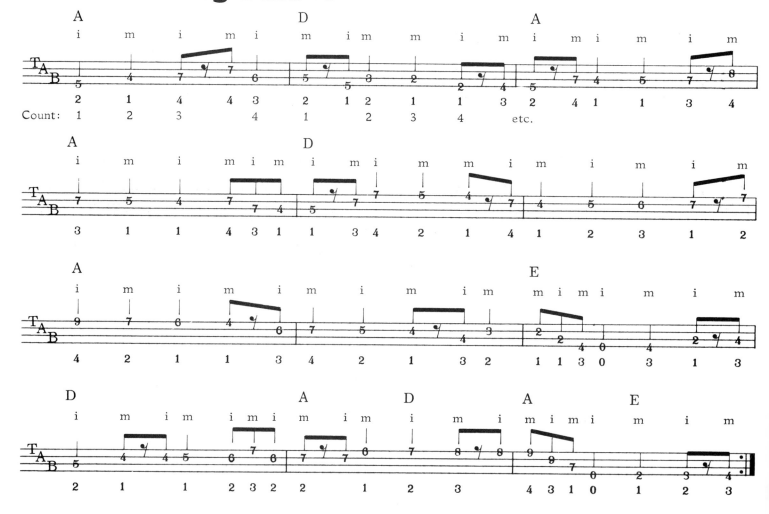

Some walking bass lines are so brilliantly conceived that they out-shine the song they are supporting. The next bass line in the style of Noel Redding (of the late Jimi Hendrix Experience) is so distinctive that it was imitated by no less than ten major rock groups in their recordings of the beautiful *Hey, Joe.* The chord progression is not included on the record so play it simply as an exercise. It sounds best at a fast tempo (speed).

Walking Bass #4

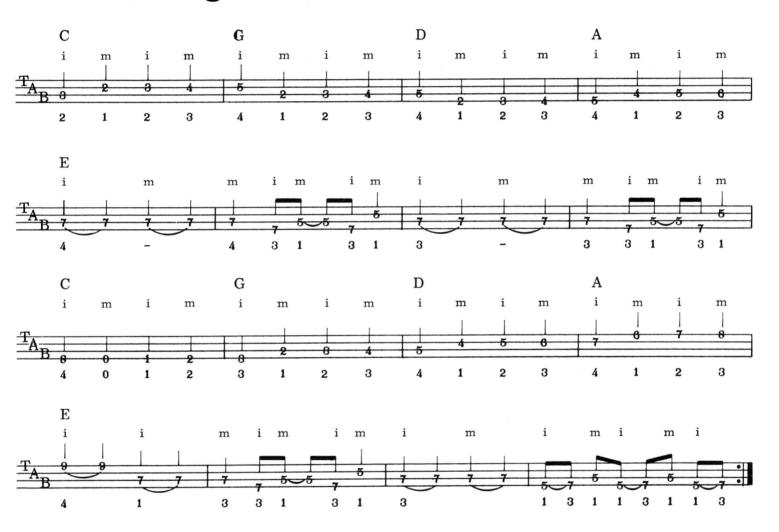

TRANSPOSITION

By now you might think that all rock songs consist of a blues progression played in the key of A. Although A is a favorite key for the blues, there are several other common blues keys. To begin with, the key of a blues progression is determined by the first chord in the progression. In the A blues progression the first chord is A. In the chord structure of a C blues progression the first chord is C.

Blues in C

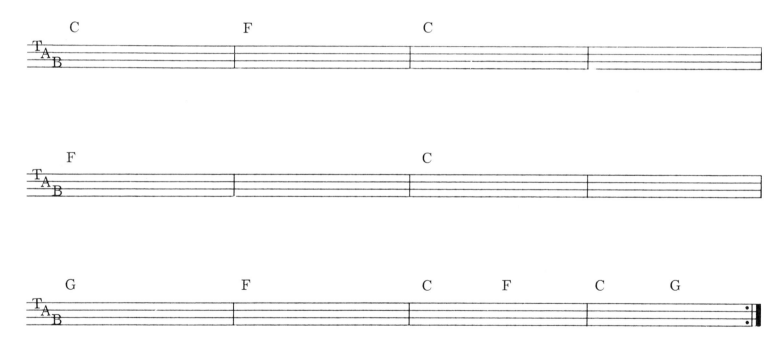

By knowing the notes produced by the 4th string, you can play the blues in any key. Examine the illustrated note chart:

When you fret behind the 3rd fret the 4th string produces the note G; behind the 5th fret the 4th string produces the note A; behind the 8th fret C; behind the 10th fret D; etc. Try going up and down the 4th string a few times playing and naming the notes out loud.

NOTES PRODUCED ON 4th STRING

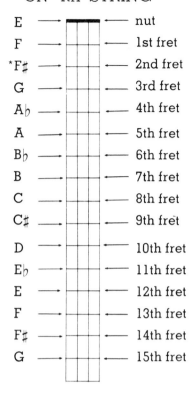

E	nut
F	1st fret
*F♯	2nd fret
G	3rd fret
A♭	4th fret
A	5th fret
B♭	6th fret
B	7th fret
C	8th fret
C♯	9th fret
D	10th fret
E♭	11th fret
E	12th fret
F	13th fret
F♯	14th fret
G	15th fret

Since the first note of the bass line determines the key of the blues progression, it's a simple matter to play any of the bass lines you know in a different key. Here's an excerpt of a bass line written for a blues progression in the key of A.

To play this bass line in the key of C, first locate C on the 4th string (8th fret). By moving the entire bass line up three frets you can play it in C. Play the bass line with the same fingering, phrasing, etc. as the original. The bass line is just played three frets higher.

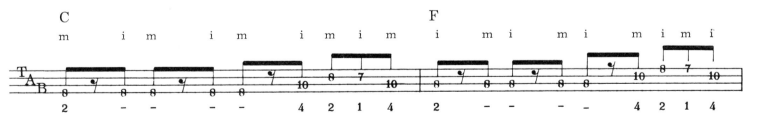

* # is a sharp. Sharps are one fret higher on the fingerboard than a note of the same letter name. For example, F is produced by fretting the 4th string at the 1st fret whereas F# is at the 2nd fret. ♭ is a flat. Flats are one fret lower on the fingerboard than a note of the same letter name. For example, B is on the 7th fret of the 4th string while Bb is on the 6th fret.

To play the same bass line in the key of G, first locate G on the 4th string (3rd fret). Then play the bass line starting at that fret.

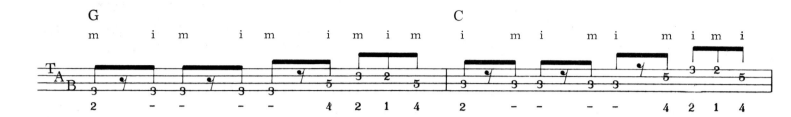

Since the chord backgrounds for the blues in C and G are not included on the record, you might get your friendly guitar player to help you out.

Blues in C

C /F7 /C /C7 /F7 /F7 /C /C /G7 /F7 /C F7/C G7 //

Blues in G

G /C7 /G /G7 /C7 /C7 /G /G /D7 /C7 /G C7/G D7 //

Locating the blues scale in these new keys is also determined by the notes produced by the 4th string. The A blues scale is played starting at the 5th fret of the 4th string which produces the note A. To locate the starting note of the C blues scale, find C on the 4th string (8th fret) and start the scale at that fret. Use the same left hand fingering.

C Blues Scale

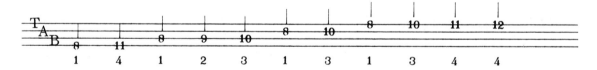

The C and the A blues scales are visually identical:

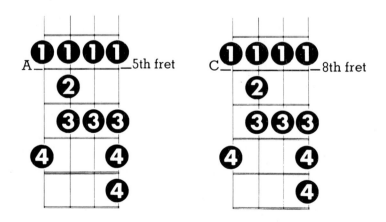

Try some of the scale exercises you know using the C blues scale.

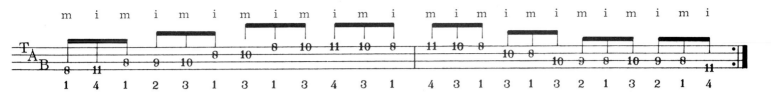

In a similar manner, work with the G blues scale.

G Blues Scale

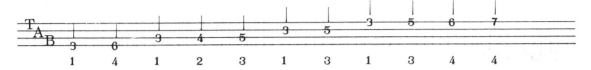

Another important blues scales to have in your fingers is the E blues scale. Locate E on the 4th string (12 fret) and wail.

E Blues Scale #1

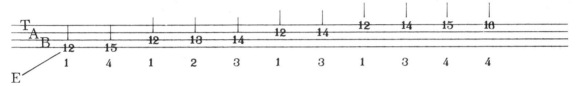

This scale can also be effectively played starting with the 4th string open.

E Blues Scale #2

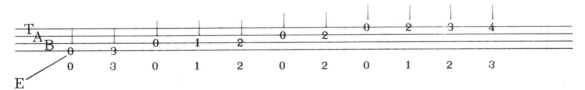

The F blues scale is also important to practice.

F Blues Scale

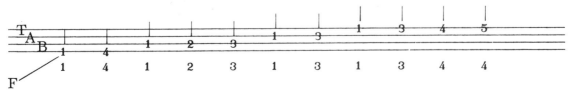

Often blues scales are played starting on the 3rd string. Examine the note chart:

The letters (A, Bb, B, C, etc.) stand for the notes produced by the 3rd string at various frets. For example, the 3rd string open produces the note A; when you push down behind the 1st fret the 3rd string produces Bb; behind the 3rd fret the 3rd string produces C; etc.

NOTES PRODUCED
ON THE 3rd STRING

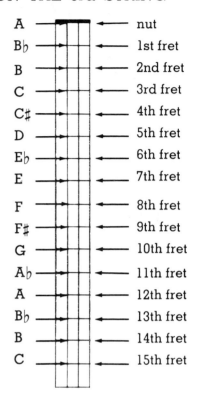

A	nut
Bb	1st fret
B	2nd fret
C	3rd fret
C♯	4th fret
D	5th fret
Eb	6th fret
E	7th fret
F	8th fret
F♯	9th fret
G	10th fret
Ab	11th fret
A	12th fret
Bb	13th fret
B	14th fret
C	15th fret

Blues scales can be effectively played starting on the 3rd string. Try this one in C:

C Blues Scale

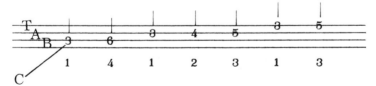

Play the triplet exercise a few times to further familiarize yourself with this scale.

Triplet Exercise in C

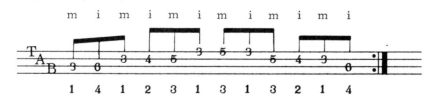

By knowing the notes produced by the 3rd string, you can play this version of the blues scale in any key. For example, to play the blues scale in G, first locate G on the 3rd string (10th fret). Then play the scale with the same left and right hand fingerings you used with the C blues scale.

G Blues Scale

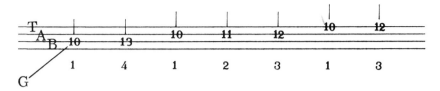

Try the triplet exercise in G. Again, use the same left and right hand fingerings.

Triplet Exercise in G

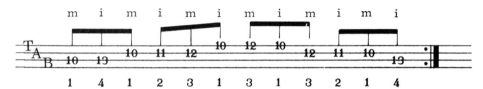

Other important blues scales to be familiar with are D, E, Bb, and F.

Blues Scale in D

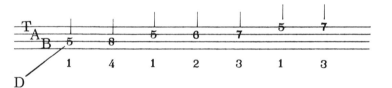

Blues Scale in E

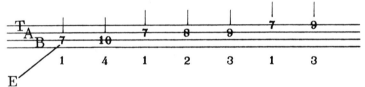

Blues Scale in B♭

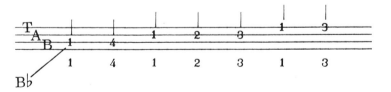

Blues Scale in F

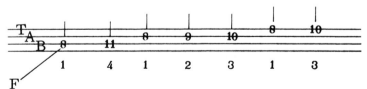

The A blues scale has a different left hand fingering when it begins on the 3rd string open.

A Blues Scale

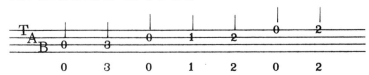

The triplet exercise is likewise altered.

Triplet Exercise in A

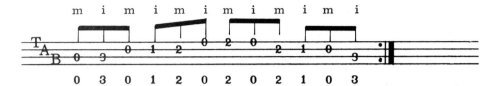

Frequently bass players will play the first riff of the blues progression on the 3rd string because the physical location of the notes makes them more accessible. For example, a blues in D or Eb has the bass man playing high on the fingerboard (10th to 12th fret area) if he starts the progression on the 4th string. However, if he begins the progression on the 3rd string, the notes primarily used are around the middle of the fingerboard. By starting the first riff of the blues progression on the 3rd string, a new riff sequence between the 3rd and 4th strings evolves. Here's an outline of the physical relationships of the riff patterns when starting on either string:

	RIFF STARTING ON 4th STRING	RIFF STARTING ON 3rd STRING
1st measure:	Riff	Riff
2nd measure:	3rd string—same fret	4th string—down two frets
3rd measure:	Original riff	Original riff
4th measure:	Original riff	Original riff
5th measure:	3rd string—same fret	4th string—down two frets
6th measure:	3rd string—same fret	4th string—down two frets
7th measure:	Original riff	Original riff
8th measure:	Original riff	Original riff
9th measure:	3rd string—up two frets	4th string—same fret
10th measure:	3rd string—original fret	4th string—down two frets
11th measure:	Original riff	Original riff
12th measure:	3rd string—up two frets	4th string—same fret

The following bass line is in D and uses the chord progression below:

Blues in D

D /G /D /D /G /G /D /D /A /G /D G /D A //

The first riff in this blues progression is played on the 3rd string. Note the altered relationships of the succeeding riffs.

Blues Progression in D

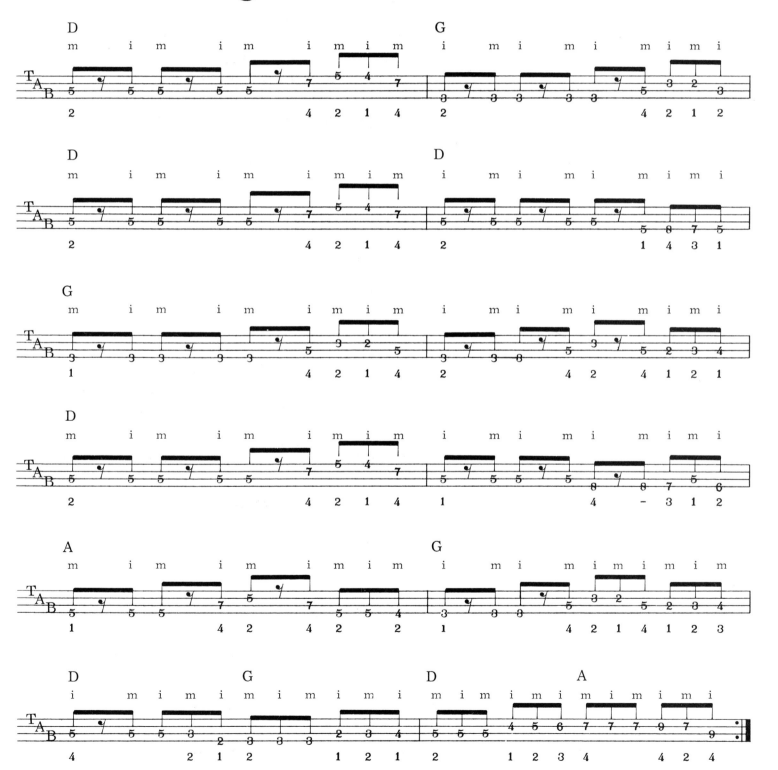

Once you realize the potential of the alternate formula of executing the blues progression, you'll be able to enhance your lines by drawing from either source at will. The following is an example of this technique —the last eight bars of the preceeding blues.

Blues Progression in D

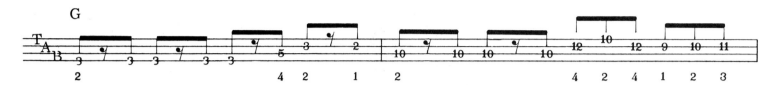

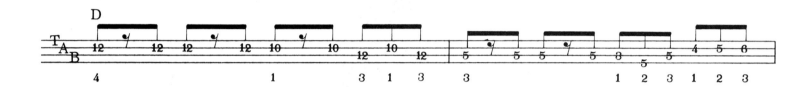

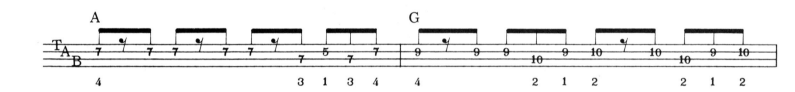

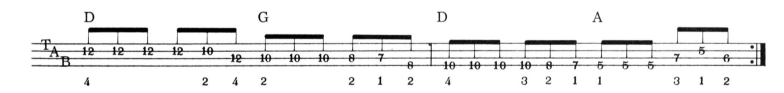

SOUL
(Detroit, Motown, Nashville, Muscle Shoals)
FUNK SOUNDS

Soul* music is rhythmically oriented. The texture of the music involves a high degree of rhythmic integration revolving around a basic beat. In soul tunes you'll find the drummer playing a consistent and highly energetic pattern; the guitarist enforcing the beat with tight chops and easily identifiable licks; the horns adding occasional punches and short melodic transitions; with the bass player adding to the rhythmic interest as well as supplying much of the melodic movement. Even the style of singing is more rhythmic than melodic. The bass player is more "in front" in soul music than in any other style.

Listen to the last cut on side two of the enclosed record entitled *Soul Progression in E.* Play the following line with the record to get a feel for the chord movement of this new progression. In the sixth measure, the A note on the 2nd string is indicated.

Soul Progression in E #1

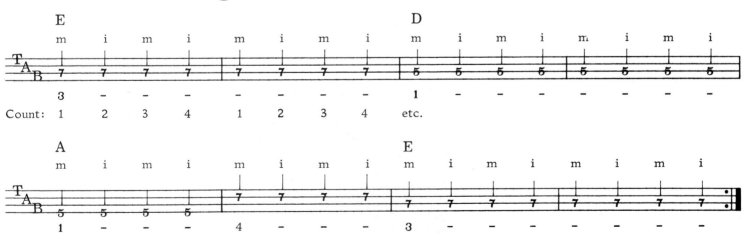

---

* Soul *is defined in Eugene Landy's* The Underground Dictionary *as "an inherent quality Black people feel they have and whites rarely do." You take it from there.*

Many soul bass lines are derived from a basic one measure riff. Learn this one:

With this one measure riff you can execute an entire bass line. Simply move the riff to a new starting position each time the chords change. The starting note of the riff is determined by the letter name of the chord. Since you now know (I hope) the notes produced by the 3rd and 4th strings, there should be few problems.

Soul Progression in E #2

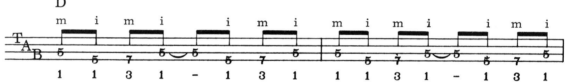

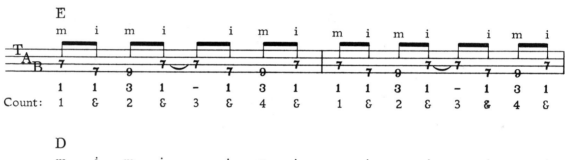

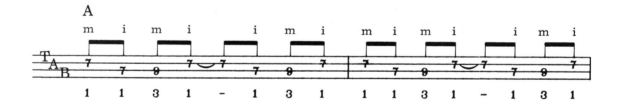

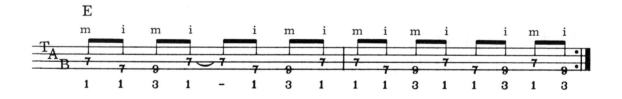

Here's a variation of the last riff. Both of these riffs have been used many times in hit soul recordings. Plug it into the formula and wail!

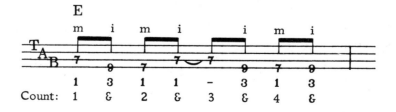

Because of the elaborate rhythmic emphasis of soul music, it's necessary to learn a new note value: the sixteenth note.

First, play this important rock scale known as the 6th scale using quarter notes. Recall that quarter notes are played one on each beat and are identified by a single stem.

E 6th Scale

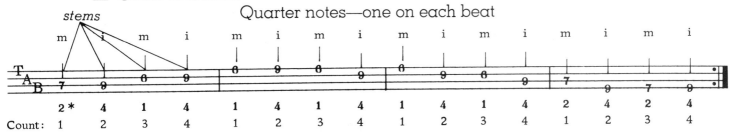

Play the same scale in eighth notes. Remember that eighth notes are played two on each beat and are connected by a single beam.

E 6th Scale

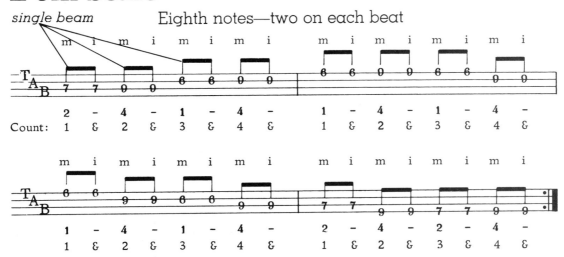

Sixteenth notes are played four on each beat and are connected by a double beam. Count "1-a-&-a 2-a-&-a 3-a-&-a 4-a-&-a" when playing this new rhythm.

E 6th Scale

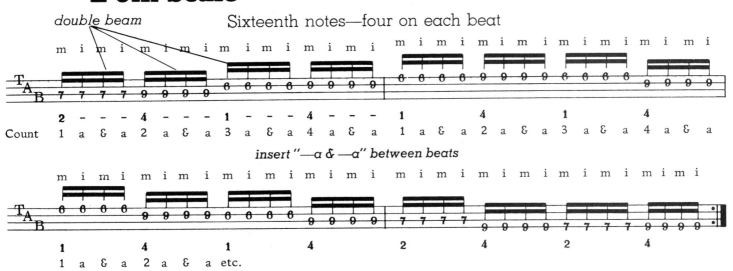

After you can play the last scale in sixteenth notes with ease, try the next one measure riff. Practice it slowly at first.

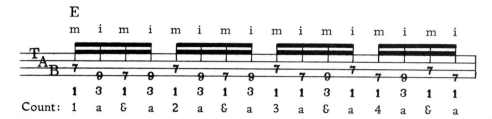

The next bass line utilizes the last riff. Bass lines which consist of such an abundance of sixteenth notes have a distinctly high tension level.

Soul Progression in E #3

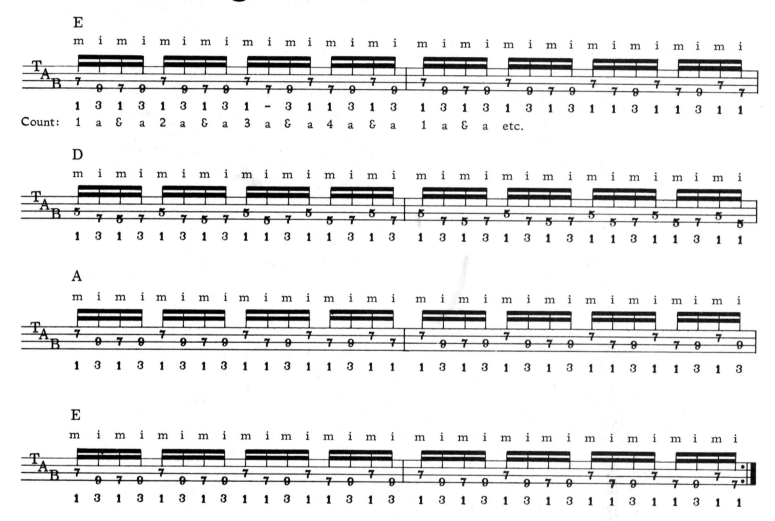

The first soul riff presented in this chapter can be effectively played in sixteenth notes. Played at this speed, the riff increases the drive of the progression. The ties indicate that you are not to play at the beginning of the 2nd and 4th beats.

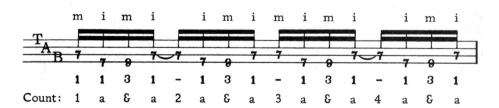

Try the bass line with the record. The last bar is a little different, so watch it!

Soul Progression in E #4

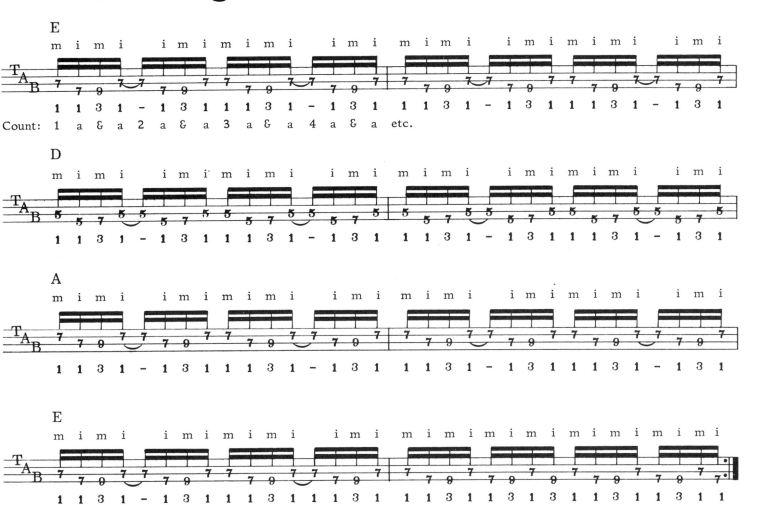

The riff variation is similarly stated in sixteenth notes.

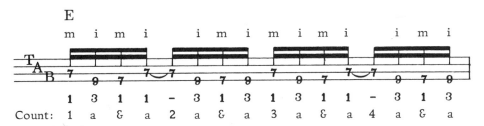

Play a bass line using the last riff.

MORE RHYTHMS

Eighth notes and sixteenth notes are often played together on the same beat. To learn one of these combinations, start playing and counting two notes on each beat.

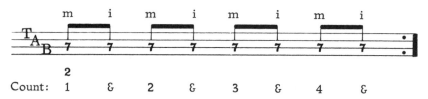

Keeping the same rhythm, insert an "a" after the "&": "1 &-a 2 &-a 3 &-a 4 &-a."

Played right you can easily hear the division of the beat into two parts. Folk guitarists often count "BOM chuck-a BOM chuck-a . . ." in place of "1 &-a 2 &-a . . ." to better feel the rhythm.

Practice this new rhythm using the 6th scale.

E 6th Scale

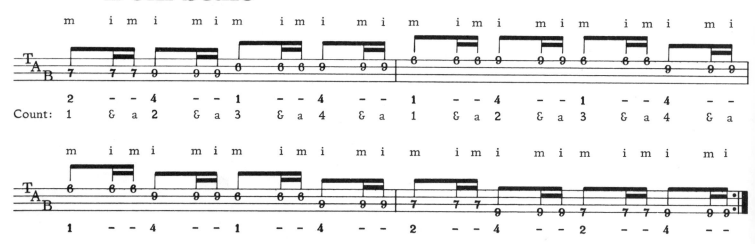

The following variation of the 6th scale is very helpful.

E 6th Scale

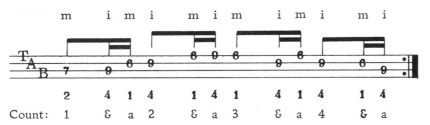

The next riff illustrates the use of this rhythm. Be sure to observe the tie.

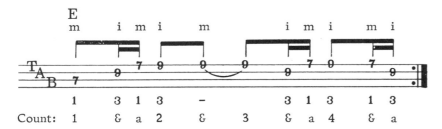

After you have the riff in your fingers, try the bass line with the record.

Soul Progression in E #5

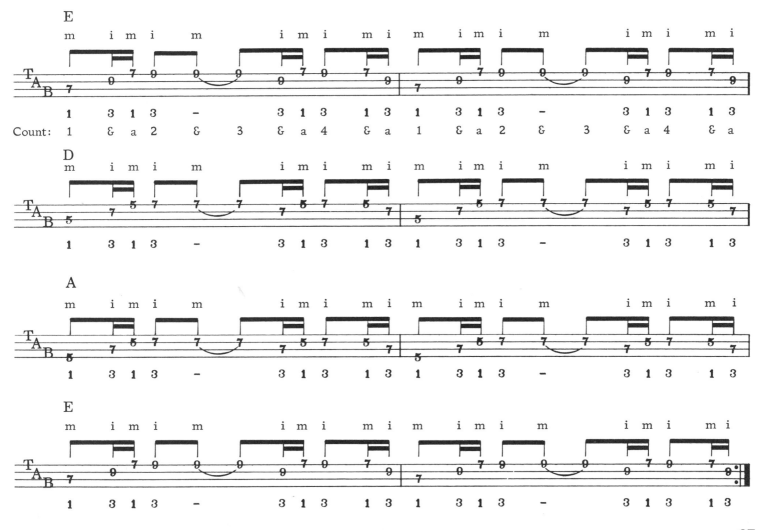

To learn another interesting rhythm, play and count two notes on each beat again.

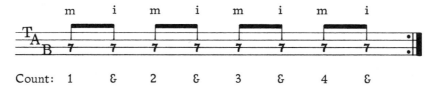

Count: 1 & 2 & 3 & 4 &

Keeping the same rhythm, insert an "a" *before* the "&": '1-a-& 2-a-& 3-a-& 4-a-&."

1 a & 2 a & 3 a & 4 a &

Played right you can still hear the division of the beat into two parts. Work on this example for awhile until you're sure you have it.

Try the 6th scale using this new rhythm.

E 6th Scale

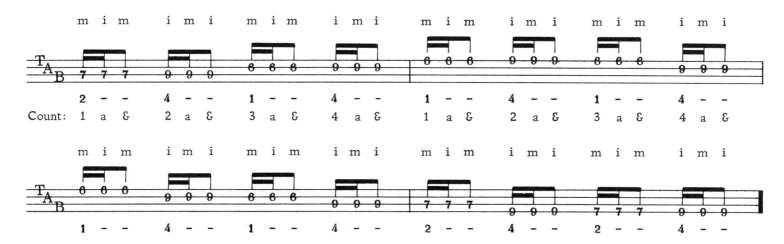

Try the shorter version also.

E 6th Scale

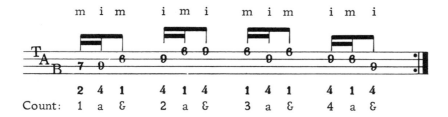

The next two measure riff makes use of our new rhythm. Be particularly sensitive to the use of the tie.

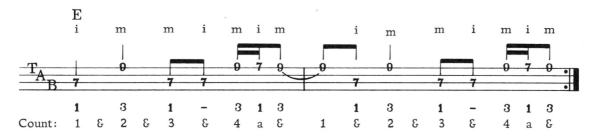

Since this is a two measure riff, play it only once with each chord change. Without further ado, here's the line. Play it with or without the record.

Soul Progression in E #6

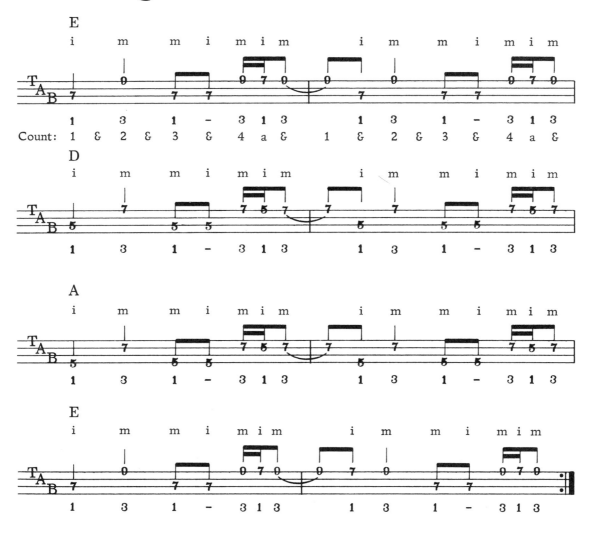

The next one measure riff makes use of both our new rhythms. It is a variation of a previous riff. After you can execute it with ease, plug it into the soul formula and play on.

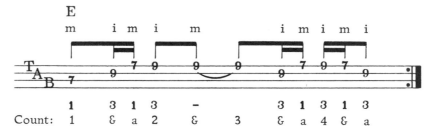

Another important rock rhythm to learn. Start by playing four notes on each beat. Follow the right hand fingering and count.

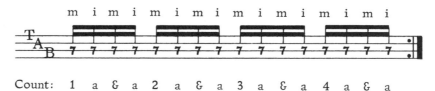

With this new rhythm the inside two sixteenth notes are tied together. Keep counting the same way but leave out the "&": "1-a . . . a 2-a . . . a 3-a . . . a 4-a . . . a."

Here's the more common way of notating this rhythm:

This is a difficult rhythm to play well so spend some time practicing the example. After you're sure you understand it, start working on the E 6th scale using this rhythm.

E 6th Scale

The alternate version.

E 6th Scale

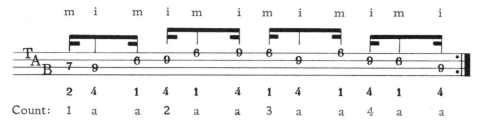

When the music gets rhythmically complicated and you have a hard time getting it together, try counting the rhythm first and then play the notes. In the next riff, count: "1-a . . . a 2-a . . . a 3-a-&-a 4 . . & . ."

In the progression, there's an interesting use of the tie preceding the chord changes. Take note. Watch the rhythm in the last bar.

Soul Progression in E #7

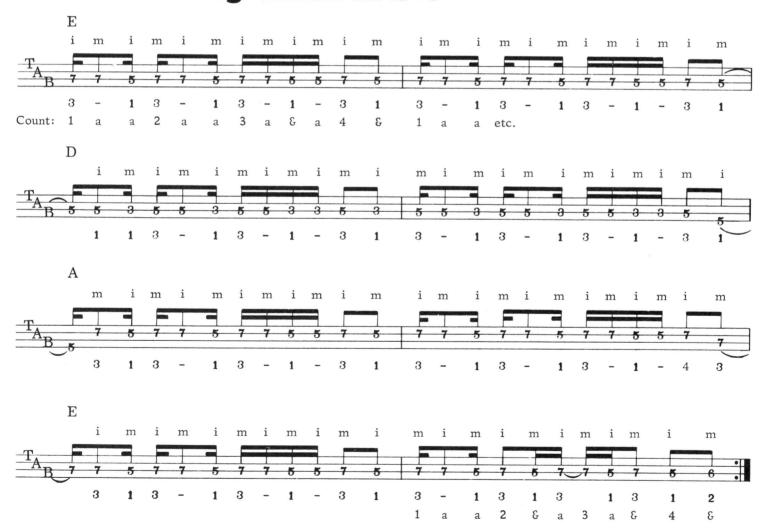

In order to play the next (and last) soul progression, it's necessary to learn still another rhythmic unit. Start by playing the "BOM chuck-a" rhythm on the 4th string:

By tieing the first two notes together on each beat, you can play an angular rhythm known as the straight shuffle rhythm:

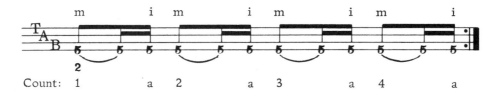

The next exercise illustrates the straight shuffle rhythm using the 6th scale in the key of A. Note that this version of the 6th scale starts on the 4th string.

A 6th Scale

Play the same exercise in the key of G and the key of D. The position of the starting note on the 4th string (2nd finger) determines the letter-name of the scale. You might also play some of the other rhythm exercises using this version of the 6th scale.

The next bass line uses all our new rhythms. The rhythm riff (remember that animal?) ties the line together. Practice it slowly at first and then try it with the record.

Soul Progression in E #8

CHORD CHARTS

With your present knowledge of the fingerboard, creating a bass line from sheet music should present no problems. When working with original songs, the ability to create lines from a chord chart is indispensable. Suppose you had a song with a chord chart like so:

Chord Chart #1

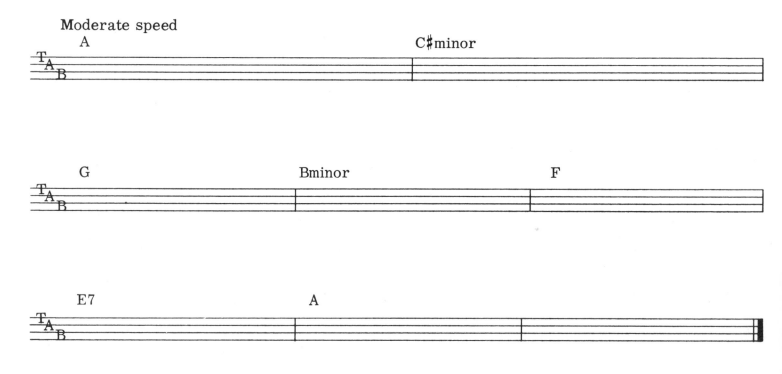

No matter what type of chord is indicated in a chord chart, play only the letter name of the chord in the early readings. For the A chord (1st measure), locate and play the note A; for the C♯ minor chord (2nd measure), locate and play the note C♯; etc.

Chord Chart #2

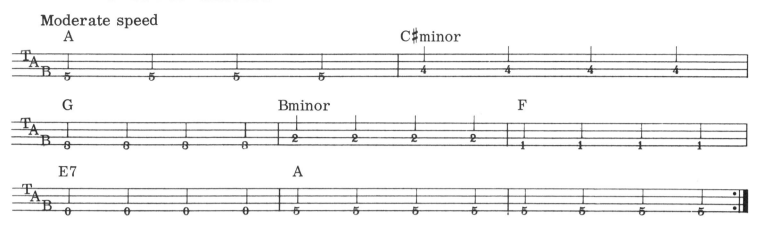

The line can be easily expanded by utilizing the "1-5-1 formula." This will give you two additional notes to play with each chord. The physical relationship of the notes is identical regardless of whether the chord is major, minor, 7th, 9th, etc. or whether the letter-name of the chord is located on either the 4th or 3rd string.

Letter-name on 4th string .... on 3rd string

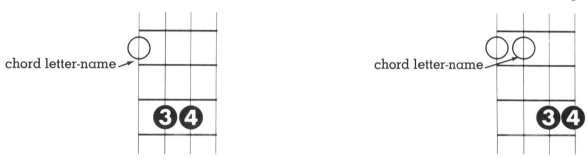

This will become clearer to you after executing the following progression. For a better understanding, compare it to the previous chord chart.

Chord Chart #3

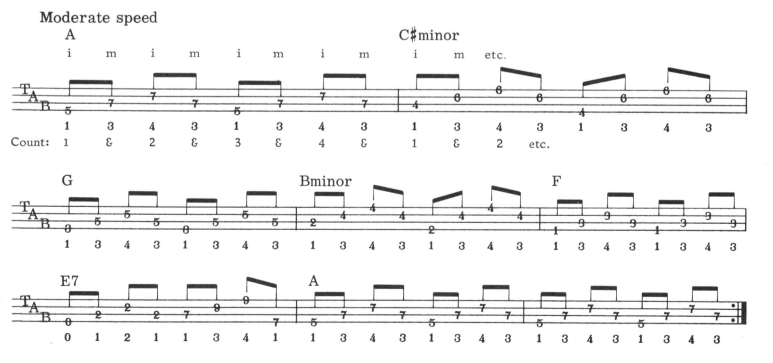

When constructing original bass lines, look for concepts that provide an overall unity to the line. A few possibilities to look for are lines that descend, lines that ascend, lines that are rhythmically unified, and lines that are melodicly unified. The line that we're working with has a descending line running through it. The first thing to do is isolate the line.

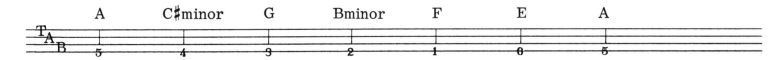

With each chord, the line descends one fret. To bring out this line, play these notes on the first and last beat of each measure.

The rhythmic activity of the line is related to the absence or presence of a melodic instrument. This means that when the singer is singing, keep the bass line rhythmically simple. When the singer pauses for breath or whatever, increase the activity in the bass. The human ear is accustomed to listening to one thing at a time, and an abundance of activity in the bass detracts from the singing (unless that's what you want).

Chord Chart #4

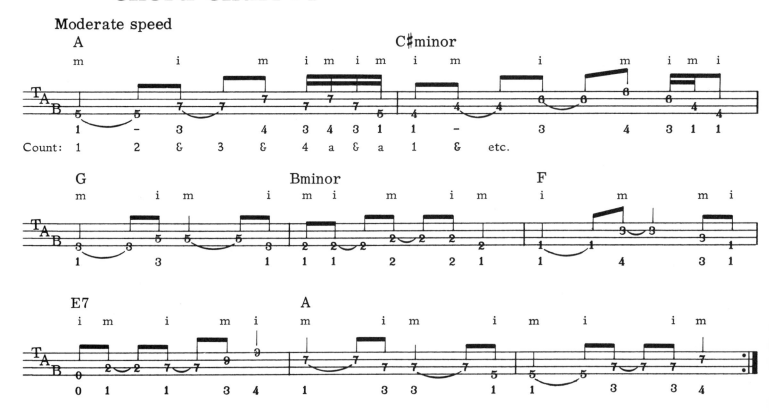

In addition to the 1-5-1 formula, you can also use the 6th and blues scales when creating lines. You can play the blues scale with *any* minor chord —this includes minor 6th, minor 7th, and minor 9th chords. Here are the two blues scales you know. The diamonds indicate the name of the scale as well as the letter-name of the chord with which the scale can be used.

Blues Scales

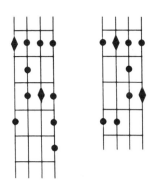

You can play the 6th scale with any major chord—this includes any of the 6th, 7th, or 9th chords you may encounter.

6th Scales

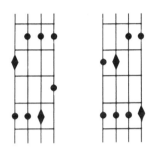

So now you understand why a good knowledge of these two scales is important. Play the next progression to see a practical application of this theory.

Chord Chart #5

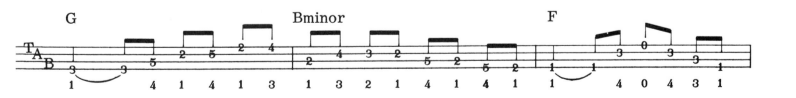

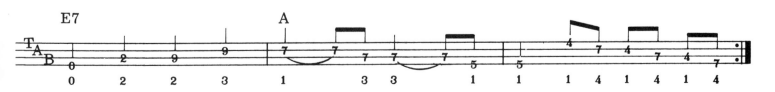

APPENDIX

Of the many different styles and brand names of electric bass guitars currently available, the Fender Precision Bass is played by more studio and gig-a-day rock bass players than any other instrument. At one time in the industry, Fender and bass were practically one word. A musician wasn't just a bass player—he was a Fender-bass player. The Precision Bass was one of the first to be mass marketed. It is a well engineered instrument and withstands the torture of continual use and abuse. No other bass measures up to the popularity and universal acceptance of the Fender Precision Bass.

Fender also markets the Jazz Bass and the Music Master. Both are fine basses with the latter being primarily used by students.

For a shorter neck and a more sustaining tone, many bass players prefer the Gibson line which includes the popular EB3 and the Les Paul.

Before you decide which to buy, try out several different ones at a music store. The kind of bass you get will greatly affect the sound of your music, so the decision is an important one.

Once you have decided on the type of bass you want, there is still the problem of getting the best bass for your money. If you have never bought a bass before, take a bass playing friend or teacher to the store with you. Here are several important things to look for before buying:

Are the frets in tune? Pluck each string open and then fretted at the 12 fret. The notes should be perfect octaves. If the two notes don't sound in tune, the frets might not be placed properly or the neck might be warped. Then again, maybe only the bridge needs readjusting. But these are questions for a person experienced in these matters.

Is the action too high or too low? Many electric basses have devices that allow you to adjust the action (distance of the strings from the fingerboard). If the action is too high, it will be difficult to fret the strings properly. If too low, the strings will buzz (hit the frets while vibrating) and the tone will be poor. If the action is not comfortable one way or the other, see if the bridge can be adjusted to make the strings higher or lower.

Other things to check: Are the frets smooth and of even height? Do the volume and tone controls work easily and noiselessly? How about the tuning pegs—are they easy to turn, and do they tune the strings evenly and accurately?

Both Fender and Gibson market dependable basses suitable for beginners for under $100.

Amplifiers

You also need a bass amp. In the beginning, there are many small, inexpensive bass amps you can buy to practice with. When you are ready to join a group, you'll have to buy a better one. It's important that the amp does not distort or blow out at high volumes. The speaker box should have a closed back.

Play only through a bass amp, and play only the bass through the amp. Always remove the wheels before performing.

Dependable bass amps are made by Fender, Ampeg, Sunn, and Acoustic.

Strings

High quality strings are made by Rotary Sound, Fender, and La Bella. Flat-wound, medium-gauge strings are best for beginners.